the flap pamphlet series

First Rain

open, read, turn

First Rain

the flap pamphlet series (No. 25)
Printed and Bound in the United Kingdom

Published by the flap series, 2021
the pamphlet series of flipped eye publishing
All Rights Reserved

Cover Design by Petraski
Series Design © flipped eye publishing, 2010

Author Photo © Manuel Ndiva'í
Translator Photo © Kotryna Ula
First Edition
Copyright © Hubert Matiúwàa

ISBN-13: 978-1-905233-70-0

Supported using public funding by
ARTS COUNCIL
ENGLAND
LOTTERY FUNDED

First Rain

Hubert Matiúwàa

Translated by Juana Adcock
Mè'phàà – English

Contents | *First Rain*

First Rain vii
Translator's Note xi

RU'WA GINII/ FIRST RAIN

I 12
II 14
III 16
IV 18
V 20
VI 22

NÁNÀ GÒN' NATSÉ/ MOON RISING

I 24
II 25
III 26
IV 27
V 28
VI 30
VII 32

MAJANÚ RUJMBA' /ARRIVAL OF THE MIST

I 34
II 36
III 38

IYA DAWO GIÑA/ THE WIND'S SALIVA

I 40
II 42
III 46

First Rain

My Grandmother used to say, "I will die in the days when the first rains come." It was July, 2005. I got up early, undecided whether or not to go to my high school graduation. I stopped by a friend's house and my brother-in-law caught up with me to congratulate me, then it started to rain and shortly after a phone call came – my Grandmother had died. The storm picked up.

Someone said, "If you want, we'll give you a lift there." We hopped onto the pickup truck, the skies darkened and the clouds were cut off somewhere far away, but from up above us drops of water fell as if they wanted to pierce our heads. On the motorway in the middle of nowhere the van got stuck in the mud, throwing us to the ground. I fell, I hurt my jaw and skinned part of my chest, my brother-in-law fell on the other side, we both yelled out to find each other alive. We understood that we would not make it that afternoon because of the pelting rain – the sky was properly weeping. So we returned to Tlapa. The next day, the sun came out and dried the earth. In our eyes, its yellowish light broke before we reached Malinaltepec.

I remember a blue tarp and a crowd of people; a grey colour on all the stones. I went in and saw my aunts. I approached the coffin and opened it to touch my Grandmother. I slid my hand over her forehead, my fingers over her eyelids, the furrows of her face were cold and gelatinous, her colour was different, darker. Could it be that death returns us to the colour of the earth, or to the damp scent that gets caught in your throat when the rain rises and returns to the origin? I remember I didn't cry. I just stood there not crying, my mother was there, and my aunts and uncles, and my sisters, and I didn't cry. A thorn pierced the vein in my eyes, almost red, almost the colour of the blood-stained sea when the sun departs.

I can't remember the burial—somewhere in my memory that time of colours, shapes, sounds, almost words, scarred. I returned to the city, to its asphalt skin, I began to study philosophy at the Autonomous University of Guerrero. A month passed, two, and in the third month I began to dream of my Grandmother. Venustiana Gálvez Marcelo, born in the Obispo municipality of Malinaltepec, the woman who had a rainbow of bracelets around her wrists, colourful beads that I gave her as a token of the places I was beginning to visit, the woman who told me stories, who taught me to eat all kinds of wild herbs and weeds and to drink coffee on the sly, the same woman who hung the wild birds I hunted above the tongue of the fire.

Suddenly I was faced with her absence. I realised that I couldn't find her anywhere, I wanted to go back to see if it was true. I arrived in Tlapa—the city eaten by the sun. I went to Malina, to the house where we used to live, and I found the geraniums and my mother like a flower in the air, but she wasn't there. I went to my uncle's house, next to the murmur of the river, I sat on the grey stones and found nothing, my feet were heavy, my blood turned to mud as I walked to her house, it was difficult to enter, to open the door, find her bed, her mill, her cooker, her dishes, her machete. I remember that machete well, it had a blue-white handle made of rubber huaraches, like the skin of a snake. When I was a child I liked it a lot, with it I learned to cut banana trees. Now its cold gleaming metal was rusting, as if bleeding and flaking with time.

I went back to the village, to the place where she was supposed to be, to the cemetery, a wasteland. I saw a cement grave without her smile, her warmth or her words. I felt my bones scatter around all the places where I looked for her, but nowhere in the world could I find her. I saw I was flesh before salt.

My body was afraid and kept dreaming. My Grandmother would come to me, give me advice, and smile. I learned that sounding her was the only way I could talk to her without being within the time marked by absence. When I woke up, I began to write down these images and recreated my own version of my Grandmother in order to remember who I was.

My Grandmother used to tell me that my mother liked eating soil when I was in her womb. "Your mother never ate chicken gizzard, that's why you know how to walk without getting pebbles stuck in your huaraches"; "Your mother never ate sacred herbs, that's why you can learn to speak Spanish without your tongue falling asleep"; "Your mother ate rabbit tongue, so you will never get thirsty when you roam in the mountains." That was the first advice I was given, building my character from before I was born.

In the face of the wind, grab the stones that are falling upon us, one of the phrases my Grandmother always repeated, a reference to people standing up to injustice. If stones are thrown, you have to grab those stones and throw them back.

Before I left home to pursue my studies, my Grandmother used to name the sensation of each colour when touching it, she never told me she was going blind, I never told her either. Whenever I came back home, she would touch my face, she would call me Hubert, recognising me by my voice, like someone keeping their secret in a pot of clouds.

I wrote all those memories in notebooks as I roamed around in many places, writing out my grief for five years. I left pieces of writing with my sisters, with friends, some pieces I forgot or got rid of, and over time some of them became poems. I recovered very few that were scattered in different books like a voice that takes root.

My Grandmother came back to life, and I no longer felt alone. There was a place where my heart, head, body, was located when I was afraid. My Grandmother became a spiritual reference and a confessional, I told her everything. Finally, I felt that I could not keep secrets from anyone.

It happens to me sometimes that the titles of my poems come as if someone else was creating them. 'First rain' is a title I would have never thought of, but it happened, and now I realise that there could have been no choice but to face those first tears.

The book *Ru'wá ginii/First rain*, to me, is absence, memory, life—that first rain became my first words in poetry. But rain causes the green to grow, and brings calm, like the cold that comes within a burn. Without realising it, I began to write to face my Grandmother's absence. In that way, my creative process became systematised and deepened a connection with our memory.

Hubert Matiúwàa

Translator's Note

To avoid the extensive use of footnotes while still allowing the reader some access to the cosmogony present in the poems, there are several passages where I gloss a concept within the verses themselves. Kunithe' is a mischievous devil or bad spirit that lives in the mouth, where there is a connection between temptation and language, as words can be used to cause harm, so in order to cultivate right speech it is important to drive away this bad spirit. Mañuíin is the land of the dead. Poem II on page 7 refers to the seductive and murderous aspect of the devil, it represents the accumulation of wealth and richness. The image of wisdom ebbing away is a metaphor of drinking the blood of your own brothers if you are seduced by greed. It is also power, which seduces even the most brilliant minds. In poem V on page 13, the dew is a metaphor of time passing on the leaves and sunrises passing. Poem V on page 25 is based on a ritual where the person is healed from fear by means of water sprayed from the healer's mouth in order to renew the heart's courage. Poem VI on page 27 contains three voices. The first is societal racism, the second is well-intentioned allies who have had a process with the community but in the long term are unable to truly commit, and the third is the empowered community itself. To 'awaken our dead' means to honour our ancestors and our history, keeping them alive in our present.

Juana Adcock

RU'WA GINII/ FIRST RAIN

I

Nìrathí rí ni'kuii jùbà'
nàkhí inu rí màgùmúu ló',
mbi'i ru'kuè,
ná inuu xnu'ndáa
níxtrígu mìnaa mbró'on ná mathaà,
khamí ne'ne rùmi' gúmúu ì'di
rí niró'oo jàmbòò ráskája'
tsí xtáa ná mùjíín.

Xkuá'nii nìnúnjgoo mbí'i,
ndi'ya ló' nandí ngamí,
nìndáò mìnáa nè mbámbá mi'cha ná awuáan ló'
khamí nìyáxii tsú'khàn nè itsúu àñà',
rí nìtháán xì'ña ló'
rí mà'kha jayóo mbi'yu xuàjián ló'.

I

You said she ate soil
before I was born.
That day
at the edge of sleep
the nights tumbled down the ravine
and my navel was a rope of blood
tied to the flight of the raskája'
that inhabits the land of the dead.

Those were the times —
we became sick with fear
our belly churned the small hours
and warily guarded that deer stone,
which our grandparents said
would bring courage to our people.

II

Mbró'on
rí nìndxá'wa nìmá,
ni'khá tsójoo nè,
nìró'oo xùwiu'
ná a'oo xphíphiú nè,
xx'xx xx'xx
nìndxà'ó nè ná tsúduu ràjuun,
ná nìjíuun itsí chìjíuu nè,
ná frìgu idxúun xàbò khamí nàtsoo jùmà.

Ná rawuàn' xtáa gixàà,
grìgoo xó gìñá ná majìúun àjmuu khamí iya mìká
—Ni'tha xiñu'.

II

The night
when the spirits howled
with a drumming of hooves it came to me
bound my body
in a ruffle of wings
xx'xx xx'xx
called me on the hump of its tongue
beside the crag of its horn
where heads hang
and wisdom ebbs away.

The devil
lives in your mouth, ethereal
between the music and moonshine,
Grandmother said.

III

Mbá'a ìnii gixàà jùwa'
xóma' ikháán ló' inuu numbaa,
xtáa gixàà gìnii,
ìjíín gixàà,
khamí gó'o gixàà,
xtáa gixàà tsí gí'dó mbúkhá
asndo tra'á xtá nàkhuu
nda'ñíín gòn' tsí màkhiin,
tsí xtáa ná ìduu iya
nàxnúu rí muwuàan nìima tsí gìníí,
xtáa gixàà tsí nàjngáà gàjmii xàbò tsí nùndii ajùan',
asndó naxí mbúká,
xtáa gixàà tsí mà'né rí mànbúmaa xtayáa xuajián' gà'ne,
ikáá tsí narmá'thoò xkrúguà rí nàmbí thá'aa
khamí nà'né ndátigììn xàbò tsí nàgóo jambaà,
xtáa màngaa tsí màxnáa ná idxúun ndxájuà ì'di mìgiin,
xtáa gixàà tsí nàñajun,
khamí tsí kùnítè',
xoma' tsí ì'skha rá, xìdxú'lá'inuu,
tsúkuè màrígù xùgii rí xtá'dáa —Ni'tha xiñu'.

III

There are different kinds devils,
like there are people in the world.
There is the first devil,
the sons of the devil,
and the she devils.
The rich devil with his leather boot,
hunting for small moons.

The devil of the well that quenches
the thirst of souls in torment.
The devil who gets drunk on the wind's music
and regurgitates coins.
There's the devil who makes you forget your people,
the one who opens the golden door for you,
and is the ruin of travellers.
The devil who offers up in a skull chalice
the blood of our brothers.

This is also the way of life
of the hard-working devil
and the mischievous Kunithe' devil.
But the lazy devil – no matter what,
you should stay away from him.
Because whatever you have, he will take away,
Grandmother said.

IV

Inuu gìña aràthuun itsí
rí nà'kha tsúdá ló',
rà'khá wuànáa mbí'i mùgua'dáá ñáwuáa ló',
ináa ló', khamí xùwía ló' ríge'.

Xí mùnguáa ló' ná mùjíín
mìká i'diáa ló' gà'ne,
inuu dàta khamí inuu nana gà'ne,
phú gàkó rí xugìáan ló' mambáá ló' inuu numbaa
—Ni'tha xiñu'.

Ikhúún nìmíñu,
mbí'i rùkue nìguwí dxàdo'
numúu rí màxáne ñàun jùbà'
ìkàjngóo rí màxanbuun inuu nè.

IV

In the face of the wind, grab the stones
that are falling upon us.
We will not always have these arms,
this face, this body.

If we must go,
may we go in hot blood,
in the eyes of our father,
of our mother.
Because on earth we must all
anyway come to an end,
Grandmother said.

Then I was afraid.
I took off my sandals to avoid hurting the earth.

V

Maxátàngaa tàa —ni'tha xiñu',
tànimbó' jún,
niwátuun jambaà ná nìtuxuu,
ná itsí ndàwuaa,
ná nìjíun xànúu nìgu'thuun,
nè'né jinà mu'ú ná raún mathaa,
asndo xó nindó' gàne mbàà àkhuiin
gájmàá ñàu' rí màxkamaa mbi'i ru'kuè.

Ni'tha xiñu':
—àkhue nàni'ñáa ñì'i
khamí xùgiin xùkuí',
màxámbúmaa lá' màraxnuu iya xtíle' táa.

Nìrakhaa iya gàma',
nè'ne mbàyúún gàjmii ixè,
gàjmii gìñá, asndo xùge' xóó
gú'thuun rí màthangiìn
màtuxu' gàjmii inuu gìñá.

V

"He won't be back, son," Grandmother said.
I didn't believe her:
I made my way to the place where he took wing,
at the border, beside the great oak
and waited for him.
Night fell upon me as I went down to the river,
trying to lengthen my heart
and my arms to reach him.

Grandmother said,
"I'm leaving you my reedbed,
my animals –
don't forget to water my chickens."

Then morning came, the leaves wet with dew.
I stretched out with the trees, with the wind
and after all this time,
I wait for them to return, still,
so we can take flight together.

VI

Xó ni'tha xiñu':
Xí mà'gàa
gàjmii ru'wa gìnii,
mbàya ajngáa wiyáá,
màgò' ìdáa ma'gàa,
kanjgó ikháán májrá'an mìnaa ajngáa,
májrá'an minaa àkian'.

Nìnújngoo weñoo ru'wa nàkhi rí nìkháa xíñù',
khamí ikhúun rá, xóó àjmà ja'ñuu,
xóó tsíga rí tsíjra'a ja'ñuu.

VI

As Grandmother said,
if I am to go with the first rain
I will take your silence
and your eyes

with me,
so that you sprout out as a word,
as a heart.

Many rains ago she left,
and I am a root, biding still
a seed, yet to take.

NÁNÀ GÒN' NATSÉ/ MOON RISING

I

—Ná xtóò àñà'
niwani'ní tsinuu xuanjian ló',
idó niguwá xàbò
tsí nanduun mudrigú mbaya ló',
nigi'ma tsinuu ga'ko idxáa,
nitagunjda mijna xùkú xawi,
xnu'dàá nithan xó'
rí àñà' ñajun kui'ñá.

I

The history of our people
was painted on your skin
when the land was taken.
The antlers on your head
were marked
and you dreamt you were fleet of foot.
Your dream told us that in another belly,
you were born a deer.

24

II

Ni'tha xiñu':
—Adà rudíí nindxáà,
nagajà xóó tsíake ná awún itsàá,
àtú'wà xaya rí nixmii,
ìkajngoo mathimaa
iduu mbro'on xuwia,
mí xùù àkiàn
maxkòo nè gìña xke'
rí rigu inuu ajngáa ló'.

II

Grandmother said:
"The sap is rising
in your bones.
Wear the cloak I wove you
so that your body
draws the eyes of the night
and drives away the bad spirit
from the words in your mouth."

III

—Ajngáa lo'
mamidii nè ná idu iya,
mastrakamijna nè gàjmàá ina,
majne gúkú ne xó xtáya,
asndo majanu
mbi'i rí mataxii nè ixè —.

III

Our language will take root
at water springs
always

it will hang among leaves,
scaling the stalks
till it grows into a tree.

IV

—Naniguù kùnítè'
maxtáa na awùu itsúu ida ló',
grigóò na inuu gíñá,
nato'ò na rawan ló',
na'ni go'wòo na awan ló',
nàdxúu rí namiña ló',
àtiawàmina' lá',
asndo ná mathaxkamàá
nima tsúkuè —ni'than xiñu'.

IV

The Kùnítè' devil
likes the iris of the eye.
He lives in the wind
and enters through the mouth.
He makes his home in the stomach
and rejoices in fear.
Beware, wherever you stumble upon him,
Grandmother said.

V

—Aganáà gíñá xke'
tsí gida' ná xoxtáa,
tsí na'kha mbro'on
na'ñà i'di ná nijambiyáá,
mawanúu ná xtángayoo iya rawun',
na nagumáà tokaya' tsí na'xmi mbi'yaa,
fróò fróò,
nagàtáá rí ngúwa inuu xnu'daa,
ído naru'wáa a'wó
ajngàa wiyaa
rí magóò marudii akian' —ni'than xiñu'.

V

The fear spirit
embedded in your flesh
drinking from your blood
and eating at your wounds—
may it be gone.

May it be captured
in the transparent house,
in the drops woven by the rainbow
of your name.

Fróò fróò,
can you feel the cold
raining down from your dreams?

That's my voice,
binding the silence so your heart
may bloom.

VI

Nàguwá xàbò nakhú ixè ningaà,
tsí judà xtátson ská,
tsí ndatsùún tsòtoon,
tsí ndatsùún iná wajèn,
ithán xàbò tsí wájun tsínguà'
ikhiin tsí nùdìí rí tsíngíná awuún xuajiàn ló'.

A'khòn nàguweè gàjmàá txárpe
nùnda' è rí màgumà mbánii xtángoo,
nàwèjè tùún xàbò tsí nagòó judiín ijiín xuajiùún,
ithán xàbò tsí tsínimbùún è'nè xuajiaán ló'.

Nuniì ñawùún nàgùwéè,
nùràkuuá xnú'ndaa ná awùún xtédià',
nùxkhaxîin wàjèn
tsí nijañuu numuu xuajián ló', i'thàn xìñu'.

VI

"Here come the unwashed
brown fern-footed
wrapped in their moth-eaten cloaks
stinking of their funeral herbs,"
say those who look from afar,
sowing poverty.

"Here come the righteous
with their slingshots, hunting for justice
covering their skin in mountain ashes
stopping the kidnap of their young,"
say the well-meaning.

"Here come the makers of signs.
They fill our hat with dreams,
they waken our dead."
says Grandmother.

VII

—Xí natiyáá nanunjgòò
mbá gajnú inuu numbaa,
xidxú' tsúduu,
mbi'i rú'kuè naganuu xàbò tsúwán
tsí xtáa ná xuajian ló',
nagajnúú náxnáxii rí tsíngínuu.
Xí ndiyá ra'àn,
àthanè inaa inuu gòn',
ikajngó mbuyaa xi'ña ló,
rí gi'dá tsinuu numbaa ná xoxtaa.

VII

When you see a comet fly past,
don't go chasing after it,
that's when the thorn man comes out—
he lives among our people
to multiply our pain.

If he embraces you,
cross yourself facing the moon
so our elders will see
you have the thorn of time

pinned to your flesh.

MAJANÚ RUJMBA' /ARRIVAL OF THE MIST

I

Nì'nìì àkuìin xíñù'
nè'nè ajngóo kaguu
—Rí mànbrà'too gé'juàn'
ná trá'in ijiàn' ló',
gí'maa mùxíyaà ló› bìyú tsí àjmà idxùù
ikhaa tsí nàxíñáà i'di àwán ló›
khamí nàkà jàguùn ìjín gò'ò xuajian ló›,
ni'thán Xáxá.

Numuu rú'khuè,
ná júbàá na'kha ràgàjaà à›wuun
àdó síàn' tsí gàtìin xuwià ló›
tsi mùxkaa rí tsíngíná ríga.

I

Grandmother woke up
in the word of the Kaguu Xáxá wiseman,
"To pierce the iron tongue
you must kill the two-headed eagle
who fills the stomach with blood
and carries away the village daughters."

That's why
the Mountain searches the murmur
of the inchworms that inhabit the skin
to scream to oblivion."

II

Ni'thán xíñu':
—Xáthagíwàn rí ngamí xòxtaà',
ká majmiyà'
jmí mambro'o nakuà' gá'ne nè,
áyuu ná inuu júbà asndo majanuù gòn' rudii,
xó naka iduu numbaa,
majanuù mbáa mbi'i
ná mùxkamàà mijná ló›
ná matha drígoo mùjíín,
màxámíña lá',
áyuu ná rígà jambàà rí ngu'wà,
ná xòxtoò mbi'i rí jayá rí máján.

II

Grandmother said:
Don't eat from the dish of fear
or your head will get tangled
and it won't support your feet.

Take instead to the hills
until the new moon falls.
Step by step
the time will come

where we will find ourselves
in the rivers of Mùjíín. Take the path
of the Mountain's pain
and the arms of the new days.

III

—Táa, gúkú àkiàn' athanè,
atrambá'taa idxàà' inuu ajngáa rí máján,
màxá mbumaa' xtayáá xuajian ló›,
wapha atángáàn
ká majanú rujmba' idù'
jmí ná xá'ngò gáyáà'— ni'thán xíñù'.
Táthángúùn wapha,
ídò nijánuu,
gàjmàá ñawuun' ndi'yoò rí ikhúún'
xó rí thánujngóo mbi'i jà'nii,
asndo xúgè' nathángúùn
ná wíí rígà ajngóò xíñù'.

III

"Son, harden your airs of life,
open up your head to the word
of flesh, don't forget your people
and return before the clouds
cover my eyes," Grandmother said.
I was late coming back,
she saw me with her hands.
It was not our time.
I am still returning
to where her silence
reaches me.

IYA DAWO GIÑA/ THE WIND'S SALIVA

I

Nàguwá xó' mùtháá
rí màthambrá'thaa jambaà xò' ná wíí rìgaan,
ikàjngóo màmbrá'aan xò' à'oo ràjuàn,
ikháán' ñajuan xò', ná nàrudìin náa,
asndo xò' ìdúu iyaa jà'ñáa xò'.

Bìtú tsíge',
ñàjúún xtíñuun nàma'
ná ndá'yaa ìyoo àkían',
ná nè'ne mìnaa xtátsiin gòn' nàtse ràjuàn,
rí nìxgú'uun rìndoo xtámàña'.

Nàguwá xò' inaa
gájmàá itsí khamí xuwiu àwáan xó'
rí mònè gamakuíí xò' inuu wuàjián',
gèjio' nàxtó'oo ì'di,
iya ndào gìñá,
jambaà ná nène mì'naa xò' ì'wíin xàbò.

I

We've come to ask you
to lead the way with your silence.
May your tongue protect us with a whisper —
us, your young,
barely a water spring.

This glowworm,
clothing the swamp
where your sap emerges —
your lip
was a blanket of moonrise,
which sank the storm
of the oak trees.

We've come to you
with our stomach's stone and flesh
to offer up the thunder of your dead,
here the blood is tied
the wind's saliva is tied,
the path where we start to feel we are different.

II

Màmbra'thoò jùbà' ná màdii rí ndá'ñáa,
màgúwi ñàwúun mbi'i
rí màne gamakúu ìxúun tsú'tsún,
nidxuu' ná brí'kháá jambaà
ná nà'tsíaa bèxoo khamí nùthaa ñò'òn ixè.

Ñù'ún, ná inuu ìmba ajngáa,
ná ñà'ún ìmba xàbò,
nìrákhaa ìdi rí nixtuu gìnaa àkiun' ná nìdxu'.

Xuajiun' rá,
ñajuun iná rí nìnbúmuu e'ne,
gu'wá ná nàtsé rìgáan nindxáa iya gàma'

II

I will open up the earth to sow your absence,
I will tear off the arms of the day
to give as an offering to the hummingbirds' tree.

You went away, down the road next door,
where the izote sings and the wood is carved by birds.

There, in the face of another language,
in the ear of another flesh,
fell the ashes that licked the nostalgia of your flight.

My people, leaf of oblivion,
house where you awake in the dew.

III

Nìgundaa mbá mbi'i
rí xnu'ndaa nìthaximìnaa tsú'tsún,
náa nìndíxii nìxkamàà anjgáa
rí nì'nii ajmúú' numbaa
rí drìga' ná nàtuxuu go'óo yojnda' khamí rù'wa.

Nìgundaa rí bítú tsí nàjínuun
nìtsikàà xuwiun àbò'
mbí'i rí nàge'e xúaa
rí gì'thúun xóó rí màtangaà.

Nìgundaa ñàwúa',
rí nàmìñuu nè ná ndà'yaa mbá xku'thun,
mbá khí'nii, mbáa bìyú ndo'ón,
tsí màxnáa awuán'
a'óo ìmba xnú'ndaa.

III

I dreamt another time,
where dreams are hummingbirds
and on the wing they find words
and sing of inhabited worlds
beyond the curtain of dust and rain.

I dreamt glowworms of nostalgia,
that light up serpents of flesh
on the Sundays at the plaza
still awaiting your return.

I dreamt your arm
fearful, searching for a syllable,
a colour, a night eagle
to give your belly
the voice of a new dream.